Earth's Changing
Rivers

by Neil Morris

Raintree

www.raintreepublishers.co.uk
Visit our website to find out more information about **Raintree** books.

To order:
☎ Phone 44 (0) 1865 888112
🖹 Send a fax to 44 (0) 1865 314091
🖳 Visit the Raintree Bookshop at **www.raintreepublishers.co.uk** to browse our catalogue and order online.

First published in Great Britain by Raintree, Halley Court, Jordan Hill, Oxford OX2 8EJ, part of Harcourt Education.
Raintree is a registered trademark of Harcourt Education Ltd.

Editorial: Nick Hunter and Catherine Clarke
Design: Michelle Lisseter and Bridge Creative Services Ltd
Picture Research: Maria Joannou and Liz Eddison
Illustrations: Bridge Creative Services Ltd
Production: Jonathan Smith

Originated by Dot Gradations Ltd
Printed and bound in China by South China Printing Company

ISBN 1 844 21397 8
07 06 05 04 03
10 9 8 7 6 5 4 3 2 1

British Library Cataloguing in Publication Data
Morris, Neil
Earth's Changing Rivers. – (Landscapes and People)
551.4'83
A full catalogue record for this book is available from the British Library.

Acknowledgements
The publishers would like to thank the following for permission to reproduce photographs:
Alamy Images p. **5**; Bruce Coleman (Mark Carwardine) p. **15**; Corbis pp. **8** (Gary Braasch), **16** (Galen Rowell), **18** (Nick Wheeler), **20** (Brian A. Vikander), **22** (Patrick Ward), **23** (Michael S. Yamashita), **25** (Lester Lefkowitz), **26** (Lloyd Cluff), **27** (Liu Liqun), **29** (James Marshall); Getty Images (Stone) pp. **13**, **24**; Natural Science Photos pp. **6** (John W. Warden), **10** (C Dani- I Jeske- Milano), **17** (Ken Cole); Nature Picture Library (Dave Watts) p. **14**; Phil Cooke p. **21**; Robert Harding Picture Library p. **12**.

Cover photograph of power boat speeding down winding waterway reproduced with permission of Getty Images/Stone.

The publishers would like to thank Margaret Mackintosh for her assistance in the preparation of this book.

Contents

Any words appearing in the text in bold, **like this**, are explained in the Glossary.

What is a river?

What do you think of when you think of a river? Is it a torrent of white water carrying a bobbing canoe fast downhill? Or is it a gently flowing ribbon of water winding between trees and fields? Whichever one you think of, you're right. A river can be both of these things, and many others too.

A river is any large amount of **fresh water**, usually flowing to the sea. Most rivers start on high ground. The water collects together and then flows downhill in its own **channel**.

Water flows in small streams before these become deep and wide enough to be called a river. Some rivers flow for many kilometres before they reach the sea. Sometimes they flow into another river or a **lake**. A lake is a body of water that is surrounded by land.

This world map shows where the world's ten longest rivers are. The longest of all, the River Nile, flows for 6670 kilometres (4144 miles) from central Africa all the way northwards to the Mediterranean Sea.

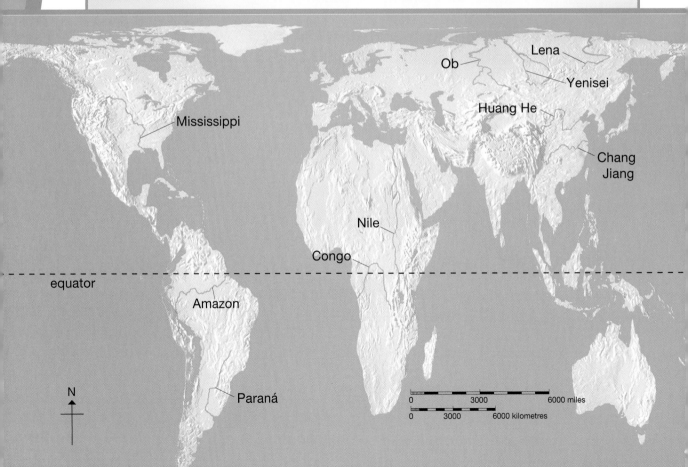

Rivers change a lot on their way from high ground to the sea. They also change the land through which they flow. The way in which people use rivers changes them too.

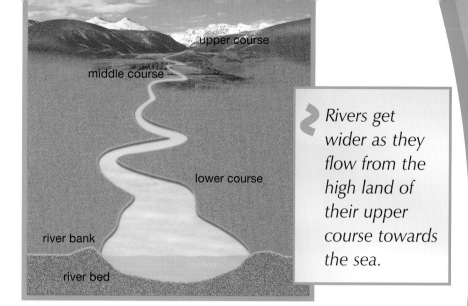

upper course

middle course

lower course

river bank

river bed

Rivers get wider as they flow from the high land of their upper course towards the sea.

World of rivers

There are rivers flowing across the land on all the world's continents except very cold Antarctica, where the water is frozen and so cannot flow. Each river is different and flows through a different **landscape**. They make **valleys**, **gorges** and waterfalls, and sometimes rivers flow over their banks and flood the nearby land.

People used rivers in the past and we still use them today. Rivers are important to humans for many reasons, including drinking water and transport, but in recent times we have tried to change them so that they are even more useful. This has brought benefits, but it has also brought problems.

Many of the world's rivers are very busy. They flow through towns and cities. This is the Huangpu River in Shanghai, China.

How do rivers form?

When rain falls on land, some of it seeps into the ground and some stays on the surface. The water that stays on the surface forms tiny streams. Many of the tiny streams join each other as they rush downhill. The more streams that join together, the bigger the flow of water becomes. When the flow of water is wide, we call it a river. The beginning of a river is called its **source**.

> The waters of the Merced River rush downhill over waterfalls and **rapids** in Yosemite National Park, California, USA.

Headwaters

Water always flows downhill, and so rivers flow from high ground to the sea. Streams near the river's source form its **headwaters**, where the water is still shallow. It flows quickly, tumbling down steep slopes. The streams run together to make a small river. As the river flows, it wears away the land on either side and starts to cut its own **channel** into the ground.

The region that includes a river's source and headwaters is called its upper course. Here the water flows fast and wild, because the land is steep and often rocky.

The water cycle and the river basin

The Sun heats water on land and in the world's seas and oceans (as shown below). The heat changes water into a gas called water vapour. This happens everywhere – in seas, ponds, and even in small puddles. The vapour rises into the air, where it cools to form droplets, or tiny drops, of water. The droplets join together to make clouds, and eventually the water falls back to Earth as rain or snow. The water runs into the river from the higher ground around it. This is called the **river basin**. The highest ground, which separates one river basin from another, is called the watershed. The river takes the water back to the ocean, where the cycle starts all over again.

rain

to vegetation

to streams and lakes

from lakes and rivers

evaporation from vegetation

from the sea

into ground

lake

sea

Middle course

Further downhill, in the middle course, smaller rivers often join the main river flow. The smaller rivers, which are like branches of the big river, are called **tributaries**. They swell the flow of the river, making its **channel** wider. Most big, wide rivers have many tributaries.

Lower course

When the river reaches flatter land, it flows more calmly and gets wider. Then it often starts to wind and loop around. Curved bends form in the river, called **meanders**. The flatter land of the lower course means that the river can easily overflow its banks. This happens after heavy rainfall or when snow melts quickly near the **source** of the river, which brings more water into the river from the **river basin**. The flat area beside the river that can sometimes be flooded is called the **flood plain**.

> *The Pearl River makes such a large meander at this point in Mississippi, USA, that it almost turns back on itself.*

At the mouth

The river ends at its **mouth**. This is the place where the river's water flows into the sea. Most rivers are at their widest near their mouth. The wide part of a large river near its mouth is often called an **estuary**. Here the river's **fresh water** mixes with the salty water of the sea.

When they get near the sea, many of the world's biggest rivers split into smaller channels. This is because as the flow of water slows down, small stones and **silt** cannot be carried along, and the river can no longer carve a single channel. The fan-shaped area through which the channels flow near the mouth of a river is called a **delta**. The name comes from the shape of a Greek letter that looks like a triangle (Δ = delta).

The River Missouri is the main tributary of the Mississippi, the longest river in North America. The two rivers join up near the city of St Louis. They both have many other tributaries. The Mississippi fans out and flows through a delta into the Gulf of Mexico. Because of its shape, this is called a bird's-foot delta.

From the source of the Missouri in the Rocky Mountains to the Mississippi delta, this 'great river' (which is what Mississippi means) is more than 6000 kilometres (3728 miles) long.

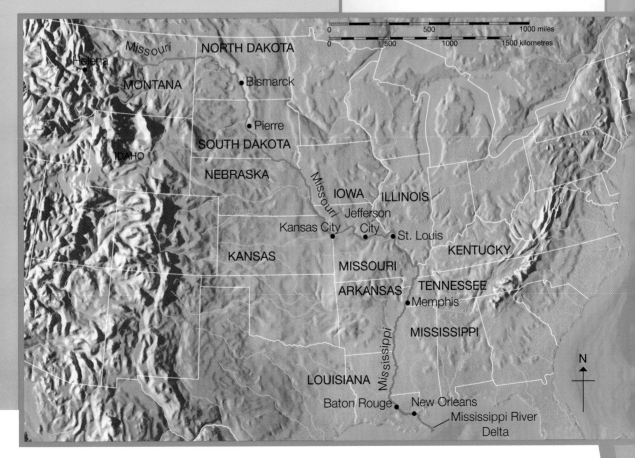

Changing landscapes

As a river flows, the force of its moving water washes away loose soil and pieces of rock. In this way the river cuts its own **channel** in the ground. Its rushing water then carries along large **boulders** and smaller stones, as well as tiny pieces of rock. This moving load scrapes against the bottom and sides of the river's channel, making it deeper and wider. The process of wearing away rocks and carrying pieces away is called **erosion**.

Carving a gorge

Erosion helps rivers carve out **valleys**. Over a long period of time some make steep valleys called **gorges**, or **canyons**. The Grand Canyon, in Arizona, USA, is the largest gorge in the world. In places it plunges to a depth of around 1800 metres, carved out by the river as it makes its way downhill. At its widest point, it is 29 kilometres (18 miles) across. The Grand Canyon was carved over millions of years by the Colorado River, which flows through it. As the river wore away the rocks, movements deep underground lifted the surrounding land upwards. Every year, summer heat and winter frost and rain make cracks in the canyon's rocks wider.

Gravel, sand and clay

Boulders and stones bump into each other as the river carries them along. Pieces break off, while heavier rocks drop to the bottom as the river begins to slow down in its middle course. The smaller pieces go on rubbing and scraping against the land as they are carried along. This forms gravel, made up of smaller stones, which is carried further **downstream**. The gravel breaks into smaller fragments of sand and clay. As the river flows more slowly it deposits (drops) these fragments as **silt**. Some silt is carried all the way to the sea.

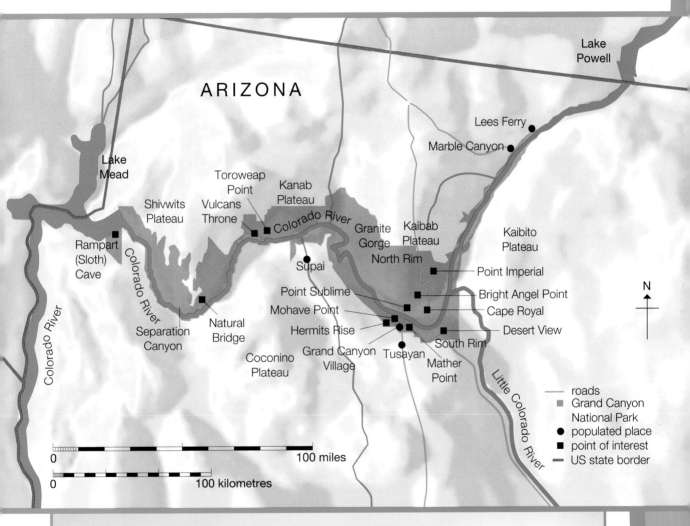

2 *The shaded area shows the **national park** around the Grand Canyon. The Colorado River flows from the top right of the map, on its way from the Rocky Mountains to the Gulf of California. There are many points of interest where visitors can look down into the Canyon. These are areas of harder rock that have not been eroded by the river. The river cuts a winding path through areas of softer rock.*

Waterfalls

When a river drops suddenly from a higher to a lower level, it forms a waterfall. Most waterfalls are found in the upper course of a river, where it flows through mountains. They form when a river crosses from one type of rock to another. Some types of rock are harder than others. First the river flows across a hard rock, which is difficult to wear away. Then it flows across a softer rock, which wears away more easily. A step is formed. The harder rock becomes a **cliff**, and the river flows over this to make a waterfall.

Flooding

Rivers flow evenly throughout the year if rainfall provides them with a constant supply of water. When there is much more rain than usual, however, a river can rise above its normal level. Then water pours over the river banks and causes a flood.

2 *Every year there are floods in Bangladesh. This is because much of the country is a **flood plain** for two great rivers – the Ganges and the Brahmaputra – and their **tributaries**. Very high rainfall at certain times of the year causes the rivers to flood, and this is often made worse by tropical storms.*

Drying up

When there is little or no rainfall for several months at a time, rivers may dry up. This happens a lot in dry regions of the world, leaving dry, cracked river beds. Dry river beds in deserts are called wadis. Because the river **channel** is already carved, it fills up again quickly when there is heavy rainfall.

The spectacular Horseshoe Falls, on the Niagara River, is about 670 metres wide and is separated by an island from the American Falls. Together they make up Niagara Falls.

Niagara Falls

Halfway between Lake Erie and Lake Ontario, on the border between the USA and Canada, the Niagara River plunges over the edge of a high cliff. This makes the famous Niagara Falls, the name of which means 'thunder water'. The Falls drop up to 59 metres at their highest point, from the top of a cliff formed out of a hard kind of limestone rock called dolomite. The water plunges on to softer sandstone and shale rock below. As the softer rocks are worn away at the bottom of the cliff, the swirling water weakens the cliff and pieces of limestone break off. Because of this, the Falls are slowly moving back towards Lake Erie – at a rate of about 1 metre a year.

Changing life

Water is needed by all forms of life – plants, animals and humans. That is why rivers are important to all life on Earth. Many plants grow beside rivers, where they are well watered. They provide food for animals that live near the river or that come to the river to drink. The same is true for humans, who also catch the river animals, including fish, for food.

In the upper course of a river, the water is usually cold and fast-flowing. Few plants can survive in these conditions, so there is very little for animals to feed on. The small amount of vegetation that does grow is enough to provide food for young insects, such as mayflies. A few snails and leeches may also find enough to eat in the river's upper course.

Along the river bank

Further down the river, as it becomes calmer and wider, more plants grow along the banks and in the river itself. These provide food for insects and other animals, which are eaten in turn by frogs and fish. Fish are able to swim against the **current** in this part of the river. Their presence attracts larger animals, which make resting places and nests in the river bank. The living things in and around the river depend on each other for food and survival.

The most unusual thing about the Australian platypus is its long, flattened snout, often called a duckbill. It uses this to feed on the river bottom, diving for up to a minute and sliding its bill along the bed to catch worms, shellfish and insects.

Feeding on the river bed

Some animals have become specially adapted to life beside and in the river. One of these is the platypus, an egg-laying **mammal** that lives only in Australia. Its toes are joined together by skin, giving it webbed feet that help with swimming. The platypus also has claws, which are useful for digging its burrow in the river bank.

Near the mouth

Many water birds like to live near the mouths of rivers. There the water is generally slow-moving, and they can keep an eye open for fish and other small animals swimming out to sea.

In the great rivers

Most dolphins live in the sea, but some have adapted to great rivers – including the Amazon of Brazil, the Chang Jiang of China (home of the dolphin shown below), and the Ganges of India. These are different species, or kinds, but they have many things in common. They all have long, slender beaks and poor eyesight. The river dolphins feed on fish and shrimps.

Fish

There are fish in most of the world's rivers. They feed on many smaller river creatures, and themselves provide food for larger animals. Some **freshwater** fish, such as graylings and brown trout, like the clear water of fast-moving rivers. Others, such as catfish and carp, prefer the calmer, muddy water of the lower course. The presence of fish was one reason why people chose to settle near rivers, but in recent years they have been greatly harmed by **pollution**. Pollution not only harms fish, it also kills the food they eat to survive.

Swimming upstream

Salmon are used to all kinds of water conditions, as they swim the length of rivers. A salmon's life begins in the gravel at the bottom of a stream. When a young fish hatches out of its egg, it swims all the way down the river to the sea. Some salmon stay in the sea for up to five years. Then they return to exactly the same river and begin the difficult journey back to where they started life. This journey can take several months, and the fish may swim thousands of kilometres. Scientists believe that salmon recognize their home river by its smell. It is difficult swimming **upstream** against the **current**, and they have to leap over **rapids** and even waterfalls (right). Once they have reached home, female salmon lay their eggs. Pacific salmon then die, but Atlantic salmon may return to the sea to begin the cycle once again.

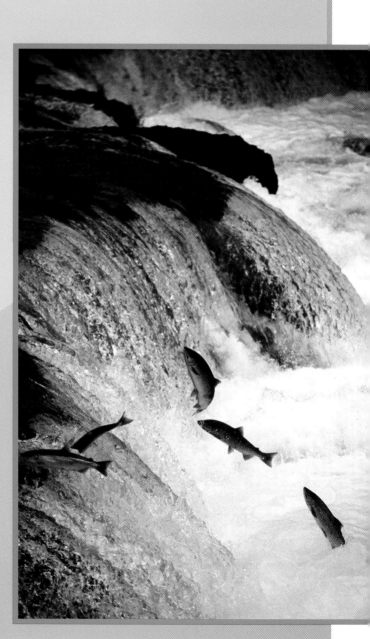

Water birds

Many different kinds of birds live near rivers, feeding on fish and other water creatures. Most kingfishers nest in holes in banks, often in the middle course of a river. They perch on a branch hanging near or over the water, ready to dive when they see a passing fish. Herons feed in a different way. They prefer to wait at the edge of the river, on the bank or wading in shallow water. They often stand very still, and then suddenly dart their head down after their **prey**. Ducks spend a great deal of time swimming on the water. Some dive to feed, while others feed on the surface, on small animals and weeds.

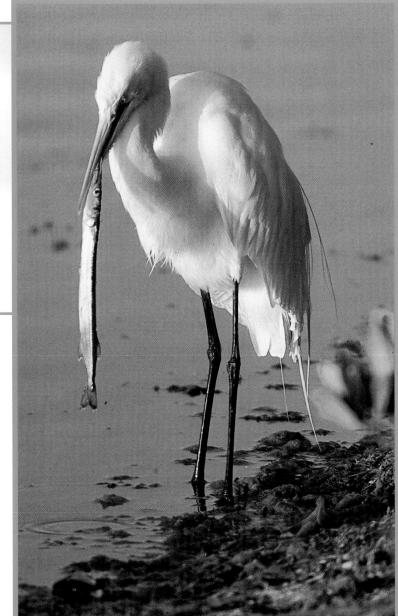

*This great white egret belongs to the heron family. Egrets often make their nests in reed beds near the **mouths** of rivers, where they find plenty of food – fish, insects and plants.*

Changing settlements

Rivers have always been important to people. Early humans followed the course of rivers as they moved around, hunting wild animals and gathering roots and berries for food as they went. Rivers provided water and offered plenty of food to catch.

Ancient civilizations

Many thousands of years ago, groups of wandering hunters decided to settle near rivers and grow their own food. Small riverside **settlements** grew into villages, and some became important towns and cities. The water and mud, called sediment, of the rivers made the surrounding land rich, **fertile** and good for farming. By about 7000 years ago farming villages were developing around rivers in many parts of the world. **Civilizations** grew up along the rivers, with their own languages, religions and ways of life.

> *As settlements and civilizations grew up along the side of rivers, they often became the setting for important ceremonies or celebrations. This ceremonial barge is on the Irrawaddy River in Burma.*

Between the rivers

One of the earliest civilizations developed in a region of south-west Asia called Mesopotamia, which means 'between the rivers'. Two great rivers, the Euphrates and the Tigris, flowed through this region, which is part of present-day Iraq. The rivers begin in the highlands of modern Turkey and flow south, joining up to form one river before reaching the Persian Gulf. The area around and especially between the two rivers was good farming land. Also, the reeds that grew in the rivers and surrounding **marshes** were useful for building boats and houses.

The earliest cities in the south of Mesopotamia, such as Ur and Uruk, were part of an empire called Sumer. Later this became Babylonia, with its magnificent capital and the legendary Hanging Gardens of Babylon. The Gardens (one of the Seven Wonders of the Ancient World) were built on terraces fed by water from the Euphrates. The land in the north, around the Tigris, became known as Assyria.

Caspian Sea

Euphrates

MESOPOTAMIA

Tigris

Mediterranean Sea

• Babylon

Sumer

• Uruk

Ur •

Persian Gulf

Egypt

ARABIAN DESERT

Nile

Red Sea

N

| 0 | 40 | 250 miles |
| 0 | 40 | 250 kilometres |

Long and Yellow Rivers

Ancient Chinese **civilization** also grew up around two great rivers, and they are both still important today. The Huang He (or Yellow River) was named after its muddy yellow colour. This comes from the fine mud and clay carried by the river. This is deposited to make the surrounding land especially **fertile** and good for farming. Further south, the Chang Jiang (or 'Long River') is used for river transport (see page 23) and for making electricity (see page 26). It has been called China's main road, and it leads to the largest city and busiest port in China – Shanghai. The city lies near the **mouth** of the Chang Jiang.

Living on stilts

Long ago people realized that rivers often flood their banks. This led them to start building houses on stilts. This meant they could live as close as possible to the river, where the land is most fertile, without their homes being flooded. Stilt houses are still popular for the same reason today. Many of the people of Thailand, in south-east Asia, live beside the Chao Phraya and Mae Khlong rivers. Their stilt houses are made of bamboo, **palm leaves** and straw.

These Thai families live in modern, wooden stilt houses.

Xingu National Park

Many Native-American groups settled along the River Amazon and lived beside its **tributaries** in the Amazonian **rainforest**. In 1961 a large area around the River Xingu was made into a **national park**, to protect this traditional way of life. Traditionally, men go out each day in canoes, using spears and nets to catch fish. The women are experts at making pots from the clay they collect on the river's banks.

The Gift of the Nile

The ancient Egyptian civilization grew up beside the longest river in the world – the Nile. The ancient people who settled on its banks used the Nile's water for drinking, bathing and watering their fields of wheat and barley. Devices called shadoofs (shown in the picture) were used to raise the water out of the river. They also built reed boats and used the river as the easiest way of getting about. Today, most Egyptians still live along the fertile strip of land beside the Nile, and great cities such as Cairo have grown up along its banks. **Tourism** is an important **industry** to modern Egypt, and many foreign visitors choose to see this ancient country from boats that act as floating hotels.

River transport

Down the ages rivers have been used for carrying both goods (things for selling) and people. They were always especially useful for traders, providing a fast link between trading centres before there were good roads or any railways. As people explored new lands, they travelled along rivers and built towns and cities beside them. Today, roads and railways allow people to move goods more quickly than they could by river. Rivers are still used for transport, however, particularly in areas that are difficult to reach by road.

> *This barge is making its way along the River Rhine, in Germany.*

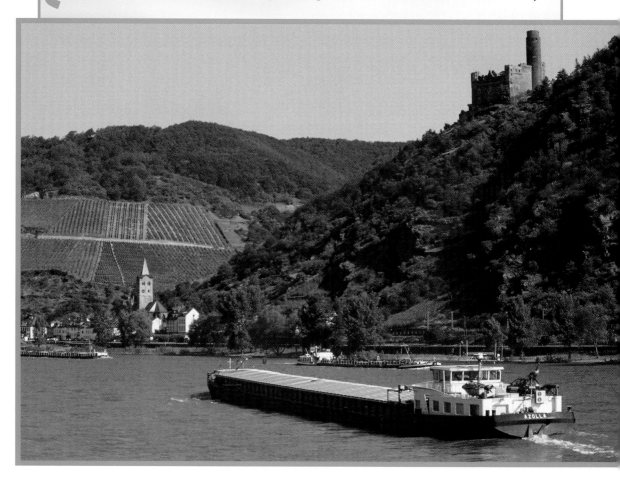

Barges

Waterways are still important for transporting big, heavy loads. Barges are used to carry goods along rivers, from factories to large seaports. There the goods are transferred to ships, which then carry them all around the world. Barges are used on the River Rhine, which begins in the Swiss Alps and flows through Germany and the Netherlands to the North Sea. It is western Europe's main waterway, passing through the **industrial** cities of Germany to the major Dutch port of Rotterdam. In 1992 a **canal** was opened to link the Rhine with the River Danube, allowing barges to travel all the way from the North Sea to the Black Sea.

Ferries

River boats are still used as passenger ferries. In China, large four-decker boats travel down the Chang Jiang River. They take five days to carry people from the city of Chongqing to the port of Shanghai. Ferries are useful in cities, too. In Paris, boats on the River Seine offer a good way for sightseers to get about. In Tokyo, the capital of Japan, locals and tourists can travel in a comfortable river bus up the Sumida River. The river bus is low to the water, so it does not hit the many bridges over the river. Many people feel that using rivers for transport could help to solve traffic problems in some of our cities.

Changing rivers

Many different kinds of **industries** have traditionally been based beside the world's rivers, and they still are today. This began because fast-flowing rivers could be used to turn waterwheels and run mills and other machinery. When steam engines replaced watermills, rivers were just as important, because steam is produced by heating water.

Power stations

Although electric machines have replaced steam engines, water is still needed to produce the electricity. A great deal of the world's electricity is produced in power stations that burn fuel to boil water – creating steam. The steam turns **turbines** that make electricity. **Nuclear** plants also produce steam to turn turbines. In all these processes, water is also needed to cool machinery, so a location near a river is very useful.

Many different industries choose to build their factories or mills next to rivers, to take advantage of the water supply. This riverside paper mill is in British Columbia, Canada.

Factories and farms

Some factories and farms change rivers by taking too much of their water to cool machines or water fields. Others change them in an even more unfortunate way – by **polluting** them with waste and chemicals. It is easy to get rid of waste by pouring it into a river, but this can have terrible effects. **Industrial waste** can poison fish, kill water plants, which other animals eat, and ruin rivers. Farmers using weedkillers and **pesticides** can also harm rivers if these chemicals drain into rivers from the soil.

Drinking water

Many people in poorer parts of the world do not have proper supplies of clean water. Yet in richer regions, people are using far more today than they ever have. The Colorado River, for example (see page 10), is controlled by eleven major **dams** and is used to supply water to seven US states and a small part of Mexico. More than 25 million people drink water from the river, so that its delta is now a dry mudflat. Hardly any water reaches the sea, because it is all taken along the way.

> To make it safe to drink, river water is cleaned at a treatment works. It passes through filters made of sand and gravel. Then chemicals are added to make sure that the water is free from any harmful **bacteria**. Harmful bacteria can cause diseases.

Water power

People build **dams** across rivers so that they can use the power of rushing water to make electricity. The dam creates a **reservoir**, or storage area, and water is allowed to drop down through a special pipe. There the water turns the blades of a **turbine** that drives a generator. This generator produces electricity. Controlling rivers in this way brings problems as well as benefits.

Controlling the Nile

The annual Nile flood was essential to the **civilization** of ancient Egypt because the Egyptians needed **fertile** land to farm, but modern Egyptians needed more control over the river's waters. After ten years' building work, the Aswan High Dam was opened in 1971. During the rainy season, the dam holds back the Nile's rising waters. This creates a huge reservoir more than 500 kilometres (310 miles) long.

The Aswan High Dam is made of earth and granite. It took ten years to build and is over 3.6 kilometres (2.2 miles) wide, 111 metres high and 40 metres thick at the top.

Benefits and problems

Water stored in the reservoir is used to irrigate (water) farmland during dry periods. This means that more crops can be grown. The dam is also used to produce electricity. Changing the river's flow has caused problems too, though. The dam stops fertile mud from moving **downstream**. Farmers have to use more chemicals to fertilize their land instead of the river's deposits of **silt** or sediment.

While the massive Three Gorges Dam is being built, the waters of the Chang Jiang have been diverted around it.

Three Gorges Dam

The world's biggest dam, the Three Gorges Dam is being built on the Chang Jiang River, in China. This huge project, started in 1993, will be completed in 2009. The concrete dam will be 185 metres high and 2.1 kilometres (1.3 miles) wide. Its 26 turbines will generate more power than any other dam.

Flood control

More than a million people will have to move because of the huge **lake** that will be created behind the Three Gorges Dam, which will make the water level rise to 175 metres. Planners say that 15 million people downstream will be better off because they will be protected from floods. This is important, because the Chang Jiang River floods regularly and has killed more than 300,000 people in the last 100 years.

Into the future

The world's rivers are constantly changing. This is not surprising when you think that just a slight change in the pattern of rainfall can have an effect on even the biggest rivers. If a river changes its course, or floods or dries up, the people who live near by can be seriously affected. That's why people try to control rivers, but they will always go on changing, which is why they are so fascinating.

River facts and figures

The world's longest rivers

Measured from the source of the furthest tributary to the mouth of the main river.

river	continent	length in km	length in miles
Nile	Africa	6670	4145
Amazon	South America	6448	4007
Chang Jiang	Asia	6300	3915
Mississippi	North America	6020	3741
Yenisei	Asia	5540	3442
Huang He	Asia	5464	3395
Ob	Asia	5409	3361
Paraná	South America	4880	3032
Congo	Africa	4700	2920
Lena	Asia	4400	2734

Largest river basins

The basin is the area drained by a river and its tributaries.

river	continent	area in sq km	area in sq miles
Amazon	South America	7,050,000	2,722,000
Paraná	South America	4,145,000	1,600,400
Congo	Africa	3,400,000	1,312,700
Nile	Africa	3,350,000	1,293,400
Mississippi	North America	3,224,000	1,244,800
Ob	Asia	2,978,000	1,149,800
Yenisei	Asia	2,580,000	996,100
Lena	Asia	2,490,000	961,400
Amur	Asia	2,038,000	786,900
Chang Jiang	Asia	1,960,000	756,800

Highest dams

dam	river, country	height in metres
Rogun	Vakhsh, Tajikistan	335
Nurek	Vakhsh, Tajikistan	300
Grand Dixence	Dixence, Switzerland	285
Inguri	Inguri, Georgia	272
Vaiont	Vaiont, Italy	262
Chicoasén	Grijalva, Mexico	261
Tehri	Bhagirathi, India	261
Kambaratinsk	Naryn, Kyrgyzstan	255
Kishau	Tons, India	253
Mauvoisin	Drance de Bagnes, Switzerland	250
Sayano	Yenisei, Russia	245
Mica	Columbia, Canada	244
Guavio	Guavio, Colombia	243
Ertan	Yalong, China	240

At Angel Falls, in Venezuela, water plunges from the top of fairly flat sandstone. This is the world's highest waterfall.

Highest waterfalls

waterfall	river, country	height in metres
Angel	Churun, Venezuela	979
Tugela	Tugela, South Africa	947
Utigard	Jostedal, Norway	800
Mongefossen	Monge, Norway	774
Yosemite	Yosemite Creek, USA	739
Ostro Mardola Foss	Mardals, Norway	656
Tyssestrengane	Tysso, Norway	646
Cuquenán	Arabopó, Venezuela	610
Sutherland	Arthur, New Zealand	580
Kjellfossen	Naero, Norway	561

Worst floods

location	year	estimated deaths
Huang He, China	1931	3,700,000
Henan, China	1887	900,000
Bangladesh	1970	400,000
China	1642	300,000
Henan, China	1939	200,000
Chang Jiang, China	1911	100,000
Bengal, India	1942	40,000
Bangladesh	1965	30,000
Japan	1786	30,000
Bangladesh	1963	22,000

Glossary

bacteria tiny living things that can only be seen through a microscope and which can sometimes cause illness and disease

boulder large stone that has been worn smooth

canal man-made waterway

canyon deep, steep-sided valley, usually with a river flowing at the bottom of it

channel deep groove carved by a river, along which it flows

civilization advanced culture, or a people with an advanced culture

cliff steep rock face

current strong, steady flow of water in one direction

dam large barrier across a river that holds back water

delta fan-shaped area at the mouth of some rivers, where the river splits into many smaller channels

downstream in the direction of a river's flow, towards its mouth

erosion wearing away parts of the Earth's surface, especially rocks

estuary wide part of a river near its mouth, where the river's fresh water mixes with the sea's salty water

fertile having rich soil and producing good crops

flood plain flat area on either side of a river that is under water when the river floods

fresh water water that is not salty

gorge steep-sided valley, often with a river flowing through it

headwaters streams flowing from the source of a river

industrial waste unwanted materials or chemicals given off as part of a process – often factories making something

industry business, often factories making something

lake large body of water surrounded by land

landscape natural scenery

mammal warm-blooded animal with hair or fur, the female of which feeds its young with milk. Dogs, cats, whales, bats and humans are all mammals.

marsh boggy wetland

meander curve or bend in a river

mouth end of a river, where it flows into the sea

national park area where animals, plants and land are protected

nuclear to do with a form of power or energy released by 'nuclear fission'

palm leaves leaf of a palm, a tropical tree with no branches

pesticide chemical used to destroy insects or other pests that are harmful to plants

pollute damage with harmful substances

prey animal that is hunted and eaten by another animal

rainforest thick forest found in warm tropical areas with heavy rainfall

rapids part of a river where the water moves very fast over rocks

reservoir man-made lake where water is collected and stored

river basin area drained by a river and its tributaries

settlement place where people live permanently

silt fine layer of mud and clay

source place where a river begins

tourism business of organizing holidays and visits to places of interest

tributary small river that flows into a larger one

turbine machine with blades that are turned by moving water

upstream against the flow of a river, towards its source

valley low area between mountains

Further reading

Amazing Journeys: Down a River, Carole Telford and Rod Theodorou (Heinemann Library, 1998)

Biomes Atlases: Rivers and Lakes, Richard Beatty (Raintree, 2003)

Earth Alert: Rivers, Shelagh Whiting (Hodder Wayland, 2001)

Earth Files: Rivers and Lakes, Chris Oxlade (Heinemann Library, 2003)

Earth in Danger: Rivers, Polly Goodman (Hodder Wayland, 2001)

Geography for Fun: Rivers and Seas, P. Robson (Franklin Watts, 2001)

Make It Work: Rivers, Barbara Taylor and Andrew Haslam (Two-Can Publishers, 2001)

Mapping Earthforms: Rivers, Catherine Chambers (Heinemann Library, 2001)

The Natural World: Waterworlds, Barbara Taylor (Ticktock Media, 2000)

Index

Titles in the Landscapes and People series include:

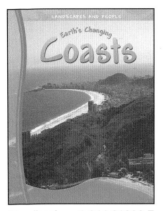

Hardback   1 844 21392 7

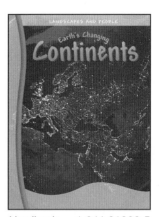

Hardback   1 844 21393 5

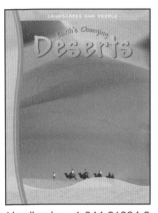

Hardback   1 844 21394 3

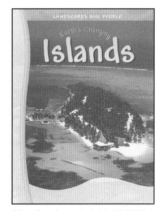

Hardback   1 844 21395 1

Hardback   1 844 21396 X

Hardback   1 844 21397 8

Find out about the other titles in this series on our website www.raintreepublishers.co.uk